NATIONS ARE DESTROYED BECAUSE MEN FORGET

By
Nasir Makr Hakim
(Minister of Elijah Muhammad,
Messenger of Allah)

Published by
Secretarius MEMPS Publications
5025 North Central Avenue #415
Phoenix, Arizona 85012
Phone & Fax 602 466-7347
Email: cs@memps.com
Web: www.memps.com

Copyright © 2005
Secretarius Publications
First Edition
Reprinted 2006

All rights reserved.
No part of this book may be reproduced in any form, except for the inclusion of brief quotations in reviews, without permission in writing from the author/publisher.

ISBN10 1-884855-41-5
EAN-13 978-1-884855-41-2

Printed in the United States of America

DEDICATION

To all the Believers and Followers
of
Elijah Muhammad,
Messenger of Allah,
without whom, we as fractions
would have no expectation
of ever
becoming whole.

~ ~ ~ ~ ~

The
Messenger
is a Sword
In A Man's Hand

~ *Sayings of Elijah Muhammad, Vol. 3*

SECRETARIUS - V

TABLE OF CONTENT

Dedication iv
Table of Content vi
Seeing Is Not Believing 1
Up The Creek Without A Chair 11
To Avoid A Trap Is Knowing of Its Existence 19
The Nation In The Mirror 37
King Alfred 43
They Thought They Were Following Elijah Muhammad, But Then It Was Too Late 59

SEEING IS NOT BELIEVING

Throughout the hundreds of thousands of generations of human experience, whatever we saw with our eyes was concrete and reliable. Experience was directly between us and the natural order or the natural environment, which is non-mediated, non-processed and not altered by other humans. If we saw a flock of birds flying southward, then these birds were definitely doing that. We could believe in it. We might interpret this concrete information in various ways, perhaps misinterpret it, but there could never have been a question as to whether it was happening. The information itself, the birds and their flight, could not be doubted.

NATIONS ARE DESTROYED BECAUSE MEN FORGET

This is the case with all sensory information. Whatever information the senses produce, the brain trusts as "inherently" believable. In other words, the eye ball itself don't think, it only transfers and processes the light which is sent through the optic nerve and the brain ascertains, identifies, defines and interprets the image. This belief in sense perception is the foundation, the basis, for human function.

Do you sometimes feel that everything you do is ineffective? Or, that you seem to be running on a treadmill; whereas, as you advance, you are always in the same place? Or, that every issue had to be fought as though it were the first one. People seemed unable to connect one issue to another, to find common threads in, say, a struggle against anything. Not even specific victories were possible, and overall understanding of the forces that were moving society seemed to be diminishing.

People's minds seem to be running in dogged, one-dimensional channels that are scary when one begins to see that this is an externally motivated attitude projected to and absorbed by all who wish to feast. Modern technology is all but relieving the people of self-dependence on a daily basis with the society as a whole moving more and more to a service oriented set up; in other words, someone else is attempting to do it for you and make the price of "doing it yourself" harder and harder to afford. It is becoming easier and easier not to leave home. Could life within these new forms of physical confinement produce mental confinement?

NATIONS ARE DESTROYED BECAUSE MEN FORGET

The white man didn't create the media machine to disseminate reality or truth; therefore, when one attempts to convey something subtle, complex, foreign and ancient through a medium, which doesn't seem able to handle any of that and which is better suited to objective data, conflict and fast packaged information, their efforts are doomed to failure.

There is too much information available at once and that the people are being given too much at one time. The population is being inundated with conflicting versions of increasingly complex events. People are giving up on understanding anything and relying more and more on sound bites and accepting them as truth and reality. Could it be that this glut of information is dulling awareness, not aiding it. Overload. It encouraged passivity, not involvement.

Our minds are being thoroughly striped from any desire to have it taxed. Digital Video Discs (DVD's) and Compact Discs (CD's) have become the study tools of choice. Instead of mentally stimulating interchange with a book, writing and oral discussion, we have come to prefer to hear it on disc, radio or television and accept the information as truth on face value. When we encounter one another, more fear is produce in us by one finding out how weak we are when it comes to successfully defending what we say we believe in, with analytical facts, intellectual interchange and literary prowess (explicit knowledge of the Messenger's teachings, Holy Qur'an, or Bible, etc...).

NATIONS ARE DESTROYED BECAUSE MEN FORGET

We subscribe to the "assumed content" or "official lines" we received from the Sunday rostrum, latest CD or DVD. This great need to "stay up" on the latest is what keeps a major part of the revenues coming in. Substance is sacrificed on the alter of cosmetics, glitter, glow and oratorical showmanship. The greatest testimony to this is how deficient the adherers are. They are spiritual skeletons or as the Bible calls them, "Wood clad with garments." All noise by no substance.

Messenger Elijah Muhammad teaches us that history is best qualified to reward all research. Also, you and I may have heard it said that, those who don't learn the lesson of the past are doomed to repeat it or nations are destroyed, because men forget.

MEMPS.COM

In this high-tech fast moving information age, as it's called, not only do we forget, you are programmed to forget. We have been so accustomed to getting our information over the media; whereas, if the white man stops putting it in front of our faces or remove it from the headlines, we forget. If the white man doen't put it on CNN, or doesn't keep it on the CBS nightly news, or NBC World Weekend or something, we forget; how many of you are still keeping up with the trial of Noreaga? How many of you still keeping up with Rwanda or if former president Clinton has had his license to practice law back? Or have we forgotten about that? Could it be that since the white man took it out of the news, we've forgotten about all of this; is that right?

Every time Adolf Hitler is shoved down the people's throat, we are also

NATIONS ARE DESTROYED BECAUSE MEN FORGET

reminded about the tragedies that came along with him; yet, like the vulnerability of the Jews, as the official story line is perpetuated, black brothers and sisters of America, we are in the exact same position as they were with America and her hosts.

We are amongst a people who know that they are superior; who have demonstrated beyond a shadow of a doubt that you and I are nothing. We have lost our value. The railroads tracks have been laid; the swamps have been dredge right, all the trees have been torn down, and today the buzzwords used to refer to us when it comes to our functionality is "jobs others won't do." They don't need any slave cotton pickers any more. They have machines that don't beg, borrow or steal. They don't need assembly lines of Negroes anymore, they have robots that don't sneak around corners for extra breaks, or sit some of the products outside the back door for a friend to drive around and pickup.

NATIONS ARE DESTROYED BECAUSE MEN FORGET

Up The Creek Without A Chair

We have thirty to fifty million people who had been doing nothing but eating, making babies and having a good time, because instead of harnessing what we could get into an economic power base, we squandered it like a grasshopper on outward apparel, entertainment and play. And now today, the Mexicans have taken over harvesting the fruit from the fields, serving as nannies, cutting the lawns, etc… and have developed that into a power base to all but take demographically over vast sections of Los Angeles, for example, and many other border cities. They in effect have replaced you and I doing the dirty work for whites. When the phrase, "work others won't do" is

NATIONS ARE DESTROYED BECAUSE MEN FORGET

used, you are the "others." In other words, the niggers are too proud trying to be like and play the white man's game of civilization. Consequently, they have been displaced. Since they have been displaced, they are left with out a chair now that the music has stopped.

In the white man's effort to kill some of us off, or use depopulation strategy, they have massively increased the distribution of birth control; shooting us down; perpetuating the glorification of alcohol and varying drugs use through music idols; thereby deteriorating our reproductive system, but they still can't seem to kill us fast enough. They believe that we have no value; in fact, they classify us as useless eaters. So they ask themselves, "What are we going to do about the Negroes problem?"

Most of us are blind to what's really going on; we don't know nothing at all. We don't know. All we really know is how can we simply grab a little bit of opportunity? We don't want true freedom; all we really want is an opportunity to have what the whites and other nationalities in this country seems to have. All we want is a chance to get what the white man has. We want to be able to go where they go. We want to be able to have what they have; drive the way they drive; live the way they live. We don't want to be independent; we just want a little opportunity. Simply opportunity – not freedom - is what many of the people of our intellectual, educated, clergy and political class desire. This is what they are going after. I even had to chuckle at a statement Minister Louis Farrakhan made at his Saviours' Day for all peoples address, just

NATIONS ARE DESTROYED BECAUSE MEN FORGET

before the current invasion of Iraq; wherein, he said something to the effect that "since we built America, it is ours too." What made this mindset so comical is that I had also heard the Messenger Elijah Muhammad respond to clergy and other Negro leadership making the same statement and the Messenger replied, that those who make such a statement is simply in love with America. Perhaps this why Farrakhan continually keeps his torch light for America burning as late as his current Saviour's Day for all people (2006).

Just like many in the Jewish classes of Germany without a home and attempting to make an effort for an existence in another's house, the musicians, educators, actors and entertainers thought they were free too and then it was too late. They were actually in the ovens before they realized they had been hood-winked; they were actually being cremated and the gold taken out of the teeth of their wives, fathers, and sons. The Germans would come and get them right in the middle of dinner. "We want you to come down to the station; you don't need your coat; you don't need anything. You'll be back in the morning. And they never seen them again; they'll take their wives and their mothers, and never see them again. The Germans closed their stores down and then, after a while, they were ready to kill every one of them. They put them all on railroad cars, and by the times they got from point A to point B, they had either been smoked, gassed, electrocuted or something along those lines. They thought they were free and independent to exercise freedom in Germany like the German people, but then it was too late.

NATIONS ARE DESTROYED BECAUSE MEN FORGET

I'm going to read some things to you and my intent is to share what happen back then in order to help you see what's happening right now. I'll show you the parallel between what happen then and what's happening now. From the writings of Hitler, and various others, who subscribed and constructed this way of thinking.

The actual systems incorporating this mind set has been and are being use today; however, today they are more refined and harder to detect. You can't just see it readily unless you read, unless you get a bit more of an understanding, unless you start watching things everyday. You must look at things in a comprehensive study versus news bite. Our minds are conditioned to be satisfied with a little clip here, a little clip there, a little highlight, a little news, then all of a sudden its gone and you want something new – again.

There's nothing new here. It's just a progression of the same old thing. What we don't want to do is fall victim, which is why I 'm bringing you something that happen back then, which has been practiced and still perpetuated. Those who did the killing is still perpetuating it through institutionalization.

NATIONS ARE DESTROYED BECAUSE MEN FORGET

TO AVOID A TRAP IS KNOWING OF ITS EXISTENCE

In the Bible, Ephesians 6:10-11, it reads, *"Finally, my brethren, be strong, in the Lord, and in the power of his might. Put on the whole armor of God, that ye may be able to stand against the wiles of the devil."* The reason for putting on the whole armor is to guard against the wiles of the devil; what is a wile? A wile is a deceitful stratagem or trick. It is a disarming or seductive manner, device, or procedure. We are warned and instructed well enough to protect ourselves, but we must first understand the trick and the tricksters.

NATIONS ARE DESTROYED BECAUSE MEN FORGET

Milton Mayer pointed out in his book, They Thought They Were Free:

"What, no one seemed to notice," said a colleague of mine, a philologist, "was the ever widening gap, after 1933, between the government and the people. Just think how very wide this gap was to begin with, here in Germany. And it became always wider. You know, it doesn't make people close to their government to be enrolled in civilian defense, or even to vote. All this has little, really nothing, to do with knowing one is governing.

"What happened here was the gradual habituation of the people, little by little, to being governed by surprise; to receiving decisions deliberated in secret; to believing that the situation was so complicated that the government had to act on information which the people could not understand, it could not be released because of national security. And their sense of identification with Hitler, their trust in him, made it easier to widen this gap and reassured those who would otherwise have worried about it.

"This separation of government from people, this widening of the gap, took place so gradually and so insensibly, each step disguised (perhaps not even intentionally) as a temporary emergency measure or associated with true patriotic allegiance or with real social purposes. And all the crises and reforms (real reforms, too) so occupied the people that they did not see the slow motion underneath, of the whole process of government growing remoter and remoter.

"You will understand me when I say that my Middle High German was my life.

NATIONS ARE DESTROYED BECAUSE MEN FORGET

It was all I cared about. I was a scholar, a specialist. Then, suddenly, I was plunged into all the new activity, as the university was drawn in to the new situation; meetings, conferences, interviews, ceremonies , and, above all, papers to be filled out, reports, bibliographies, lists, questionnaires. And on top of that were the demands in the community, the things in which one had to, was 'expected to' participate that had not been there or had not been important before. It was all rigmarole, of course, but it consumed all one's energies, coming on top of the work one really wanted to do. You can see how easy it was, then, not to think about fundamental things. One had no time."

"Those," I said, "are the words of my friend the baker. "One had no time to think.

There was so much going on." "Your friend the baker was right," said my colleague.

"The dictatorship, and the whole process of its coming into being, was above all diverting. It provided an excuse not to think for people who did not want to think anyway. I do not speak of your 'little men,' your baker and so on' I speak of my colleagues and myself, learned men, mind you. Most of us did not want to think about fundamental things and never had. There was no need to. Nazism gave us some dreadful, fundamental things to think about-we were decent people-and kept us so busy with continuous changes and 'crises' and so fascinated, yes, fascinated, by the machinations of the 'national enemies,' without and within, that we had no time to think about these dreadful things that were growing, little by little, all around us.

NATIONS ARE DESTROYED BECAUSE MEN FORGET

Unconsciously, I suppose, we were grateful. Who wants to think?

"To live in this process is absolutely not to be able to notice it-please try to believe me-unless one has a much greater degree of political awareness, acuity, than most of us had ever had occasion to develop. Each step was so small, so inconsequential, so well explained or, in occasion, 'regretted,' that, unless one were detached from the whole process from the beginning, unless one understood what the whole thing was in principle, what all these 'little measures 'that no 'patriotic German' could resent must some day lead to, one no more saw it developing from day to day than a farmer in his field sees the corn growing. One day it is over his head.

"How is this to be avoided, among ordinary men, even highly educated ordinary men? Frankly, I do not know. I do not see, even now. Many, many times since it all happened I have pondered that pair of real maxims. Principiis obsta and Finem respice-'Resist the beginnings' and 'Consider the end.' But one must foresee the end in order to resist, or even see, the beginnings. One must foresee the end clearly and certainly and how is this to be done, by ordinary men or even by extraordinary men? Things might have changed here before they went as far as they did; they didn't, but they might have. And everyone counts on that might.

"Your 'little men,' your Nazi friends, were not against National Socialism in principle. Men like me, who were, are the greater offenders, not because we knew better (that would be too much to say) but

NATIONS ARE DESTROYED BECAUSE MEN FORGET

because we sensed better. Pastor Niemoller spoke of the thousands and thousands of men like me when he spoke (too modestly of himself) and said that, when the Nazis attacked the Communists, he was a little uneasy, but, after all, he was not a Communist, and so he did nothing; and then they attacked the Socialists, and he was a little uneasier, but, still, he was not a Socialist, and he did noting; and then the schools, the press, the Jews, and so on, and he was always uneasier, but still he did nothing. And then they attacked the Church, and he was a Churchman, and he did something but then it was too late."

"You see," my colleague went on, "one doesn't see exactly where or how to move. Believe me, this is true. Each act, each occasion, is worse than the last, but only a little worse. You wait for the next.

You wait for one great shocking occasion, thinking that others, when such a shock comes, will join with you unresisting somehow. You don't want to act, or even talk, alone; you don't want to 'go out of your way to make trouble.' Why not-Well, you are not in the habit of doing it. And it is not just fear, fear of standing alone; that restrains you; it is also genuine uncertainty.

"uncertainty is a very important factor, and, instead of decreasing as time goes on, it grows. Outside, in the streets, in the general community, 'everyone' is happy. One hears no protest, and certainly sees none. You know, in France or Italy there would be slogans against the government painted on walls and fences; in Germany, outside the great cities, perhaps, there is not even this. In the university community, in your own community, you speak privately to your colleagues, some of whom certainly feel as you do; but what do they say? They say, 'It's not so bad' or 'You're seeing things' or 'You're an alarmist.'

"And you are an alarmist. You are saying that this must lead to this, and you can't prove it. These are the beginnings, yes; but how do you know for sure when you don't know the end, and how do you know, or even surmise, the end? On the one hand, your enemies, the law, the regime, the Party, intimidate you. On the other, your colleagues pooh-pooh you as pessimistic or even neurotic. You are left with your close friends, who are naturally, people who have always thought as you have.

"But your friends are fewer now. Some have drifted off somewhere or submerged themselves in their work. You no longer see as many as you did at meeting or gatherings. Informal groups become smaller; attendance drops off in little organizations, and the organizations themselves wither. Now, in small gatherings of your oldest friends, you feel that you're talking to yourselves , that you are isolated from the reality of things. This weakens your confidence still further and serves as a further deterrent to- what? It is clearer all the time that, if you're going to do anything, you must make an occasion to do it, and then you are obviously a troublemaker. So you wait, and you wait.

"But the one great shocking occasion, when tens or hundreds or thousands will join with you, never comes. That's the difficulty. If the last and worst act of the whole regime had come immediately after the first and smallest, thousands, yes, millions would have been sufficiently shocked if, let us say, the gassing of the Jews in '43 had come immediately after the 'German Firm' stickers on the windows of non-Jewish shops in '33.

"But of course this isn't the way it happens. In between come all the hundreds of little steps, some of them imperceptible, each of them preparing you not to be shocked by the next. Step C is not so much worse than Step B, and, if you did not make a stand at Step B, why should you at Step C? And so on to Step D.

"And one day, too late, your principles, if you were ever sensible of them, all rush in upon you. The burden of self deception has grown too heavy, and some minor incident, in my case my little boy, hardly more than a baby, saying 'Jew swine,' collapses it all at once, and you see that everything, has changed and changed completely under your nose. The world you live in-your nation, your people-is not the world you were born in at all. The forms are all there, all untouched, all reassuring, the houses, the shops, the jobs, the mealtimes, the visits, the concerts, the cinema, the holidays. But the spirit, which you never noticed because you made the lifelong mistake of identifying it with the forms, is changed. Now you live in a world of hate and fear, and the people who hate and fear do not even know it themselves; when everyone is transformed, no one is transformed. Now you live in a system itself could not have intended this in the beginning, but in order to sustain itself it was compelled to go all the way.

NATIONS ARE DESTROYED BECAUSE MEN FORGET

"You have gone almost all the way yourself. Life is a continuing process, a flow, not a succession of acts and events at all. It has flowed to a new level, carrying you with it, without any effort on your part. On this new level you live, you have been living more comfortably every day, with new morals, new principles. You have accepted things you would not have accepted five years ago, a year ago, things that your father, even in Germany, could not have imagined.

"Suddenly it all comes down, all at once. You see what you are, what you have done, or, more accurately, what you haven't done (for that was all that was required of most of us: that we do nothing). You remember those early meetings of your department in the university when, if one had stood, others would have stood, perhaps, but no one stood. A small matter, a matter of hiring this man or that, and you hired this one rather than that. You remember everything now, and your heart breaks. Too late. You are compromised beyond repair.

"What then? You must then shoot yourself. A few did. Or 'adjust' your principles. Many tried, and some, I suppose, succeeded; not I, however. Or learn to live the rest of your life with your shame. This last is the nearest there is, under the circumstances, to heroism: shame. Many Germans became this poor kind of hero, many more, I think, than the world knows or cares to know."

"I can tell you," my colleague went on, "of a man in Leipzig, a judge. He was not a Nazi, except nominally, but he certainly wasn't an anti-Nazi. He was just-a judge. In '42 or '43 early '43 I think it was, a Jew was tried before him in a case involving, but only incidentally, relations with an 'Aryan' woman. This was 'race injury,' something the Party was especially anxious to punish. In the case at bar, however, the judge had the power to convict the man of a 'nonracial' charge, in the judge's opinion, and so, as an honorable judge, he acquitted him. Of course, the Party seized the Jew as soon as he left the courtroom."

"And the judge?"

"Yes, the judge. He could not get the case off his conscience-a case mind you, in which he had acquitted an innocent man. He thought that he should have convicted him and saved him from the Party, but how could he have convicted an innocent man? The thing preyed on him more and more, and he had to talk about it, first to his family, then to his friends, and then to acquaintances. (That's how I heard about it.) After the '44 Putsch they arrested him. After that, I don't know."

I said nothing.

"Once the war began," my colleague continued, "resistance, protest, criticism, complaint, all carried with them a multiplied likelihood of the greatest punishment. Mere lack of enthusiasm, or failure to show it in public, was 'defeatism.' You assumed that there were lists of those who would be 'dealt with' later, after the victory. Goebbels was very clever here, too. He continually promised a 'victory orgy' to 'take care of' those who thought that their 'treasonable attitude' had escaped notice. And he meant it; that was not just propaganda. And that was enough to put an end to all uncertainty.

NATIONS ARE DESTROYED BECAUSE MEN FORGET

"Once the war began, the government could do anything 'necessary' to win it; so it was with the 'final solution of the Jewish problem,' which the Nazis always talked about but never dared undertake, not even the Nazis, until war and its 'necessities' gave them the knowledge that they could get away with it. The people abroad who thought that war against Hitler would help the Jews were wrong. And the people in Germany who, once the war had begun, still thought of complaining, protesting, resisting, were betting on Germany's losing the war. It was a long bet. Not many made it."

The Nation In The Mirror

The Messenger writes, "Now all must realized that the one and only reason why this evil race have so much power and prevails is entirely due to the same reason why bad men and evil conditions prevail, it is because good men do nothing about it." That's why it's still alive, because those who can do, won't do. "They keep on re-tolerating intolerance and pursuing their own selfish interest."

Let me read that again, "...they keep onward, they don't turn back and check these things, they keep onward tolerating intolerance and pursuing their own selfish interest; it is as simple as that and nothing else."

Nations Are Destroyed Because Men Forget

Now this is what the Messenger of Allah said; therefore the situation is this, it is up to you and I. The only ones gaining from the general distress of disunity is the white Caucasian race. They're the only ones who benefit. Could anything be so cowardly or stupid as to actually tolerate those who would destroy us for all times; we can't keep putting up with it. The only way you can attack a culture, is to build one yourself. You cannot fight a culture without a culture; you need a culture; you need a way of life of common thinking upon which we could at least circle the wagons. If we have to come to the table of integration, we should do so as animals come down to a water hole. We drink a little water and do business, but when the sun goes down, sparrows go home with sparrows, and robins go back with robins. You don't see a gazelle and a zebra walking off together with the intention of mating.

The intention to eliminate the Jewish people of Germany are similar to those possessed by the white man of America. They are using the same tactics on us right now. In many of the major cities, freeways are being used to separate communities. They are being used where there use to be grassy knolls. Solid concrete walls which go straight up are replacing them. You can hardly get to the east side of Los Angeles unless you come through the underpass. If they shut these down, you could not know what's going on the other side of the city.

Hitler used these separators to protect the Jews from riots, protesters and violence for which he was responsible for creating for the Jew. They started closing off these gates

NATIONS ARE DESTROYED BECAUSE MEN FORGET

to protect them; they called them cal de sac's or blind alleys, where there's no way out unless you go through check points, and they made them think they were being protected.

Jewish leaders were used to perpetuate the myth and was in fact playing along with the game; there were local officials and high officials. Many of the people willfully went along with it, but all the time, these people had been subtly concentrated; and this is what's happening in our communities right now. Let me tell you why they're doing this, this is only one of many reasons

I am reading from what's called the King Alfred Plan. Listen to this brothers and sisters:

MEMPS.COM

(The United States Government's Plan to Exterminate the Entire Black Population of America in Time of National Crisis or Emergency) by The Federal Emergency Management Agency (FEMA)

NATIONS ARE DESTROYED BECAUSE MEN FORGET

KING ALFRED

"In the even of wide spread and continuing coordinated racial disturbances in the United States, KING ALFRED, at the discretion of the presidents to put into action immediately.

Participating Federal Agencies: the National Security Council, the Central Intelligence Agency, Federal Bureau of Investigation, Department of Justice, Department of Defense, Department of Interior.

Participating Local Agencies, under Federal jurisdiction: National Guard Units, State Police.

NATIONS ARE DESTROYED BECAUSE MEN FORGET

Participating Local Agencies, under Federal jurisdiction: city Police, and County Police.

Memo: National Security Council:

Even before 1954, when the Supreme Court of the United States of America declared unconstitutional separate educational, recreational facilities, racial unrest and discord had become very nearly a part of the American way of life. But that way of life was repugnant to most Americans. Since 1954, however that unrest and discord have broken out into wide spread violence which have increasingly have placed the peace and stability of the nation in dire jeopardy. This violence has resulted in lose of life, limb and property. And has cost the tax payers of this nation billions of dollars. And the end is not yet in sight.

This same violence, has raised the tremendously grave question as whether the races can ever live in peace with each other. Each passing month has brought new intelligence that, despite laws passed to elevate the condition of the Minority they are still not satisfied. Demonstrations and rioting have become part of a familiar scene. Troops have been called out in city after city across the land and our image as a world leader severely damaged. Our enemies press closer seeking the advantage possible at a time during one of these out-breaks of violence. The Minority has adaptation almost military posture to gain its objectives which are not clear to most Americans. It is expected therefore, that when those objectives are denied the Minority, racial war must considered inevitable. When that Emergency comes we must expect the total involvement of all 22 million members of the Minority, men, women, and children. For once this project is launched, its goal is to terminate once and for all the Minority threat to the whole of American society and indeed the Free World.

Chairman National Security Council

*KING ALFRED: King of England, 849-899.

"Preliminary Memo: Department of Interior

Under KING ALFRED, the nation has been divided into *10 regions. In case of Emergency, Minority members will be evacuated from the cities by federalized National Guard units, local and state police, and if necessary, by units of the regular armed forces using public and military transportation and detained in near by military installations until a further course of action has been decided. (1) Capitol Region [D.C.], (2) Northeast Region, (3) Southeast Region, (4) Great Lakes Region, (5) South Central Region, (6) Deep South Region I, (7) Deep South Region II, (8) Great Planes/Rocky Mountains Region, (9) Southwest Region, (10) A & B West Coast Region. No attempt will be made to seal off the Canadian and Mexican borders.

Combined Memo: Department of Justice, Federal Bureau of Investigation, Central Intelligence Agency

There are 12 major Minority organizations and all are familiar to the 22 million. Dossiers have been compiled on the leaders of the organizations and can be

NATIONS ARE DESTROYED BECAUSE MEN FORGET

studied in Washington. The material contained in the dossiers and our threat to reveal that material has considerable held in check the activities of some of the leaders. Leaders who do not have such useable material in their dossiers have been approached to take government posts mostly as ambassadors and primarily in African countries. The promise of these positions also has materially contributed to the temporary slow down of Minority activities. However, we do not expect these slow-downs to be of long duration as there are always new decadent elements joining these organization with the potential power to replace the old leaders. All organizations and there leaders are under constant 24 hours surveillance.

The organizations are:

(1) The Black Muslims, (2) Student Non-Violent Coordinating Committee, (3) Congress of Racial Equality, (4) the Uhuru Movement, (5) the Group on Advanced Leadership (GOAL), (6) The Freedom Now Party, (7) United Black Nationalists of America, (8) The New Pan-African Movement, (9) Southern Christian Leadership conference, (10) The National Urban League, (11) The National Association for the Advancement of Colored People, (12) The Committee on Racial and Religious Progress.

NOTE: At the appropriate time, to be designated by the president, the leaders of some of these organizations are to be detained only when it is clear that they can not prevent the Emergency working with public officials during the first critical hours. All other leaders are to be detained at once. Compiled lists of Minority leaders have been readied at the National Data Computer Center. It is necessary

*Rex 84 pick-up regions: First, the Federal Emergency Management Agency, after deputizing all Department of Defense personal and state National Guard personal ostensibly so as to make such personal civilians and to thereby avoiding violating the congressionally enacted Posse Comitatus Act. Would undertake to test its ability to seek out and take into custody some 400,000 undocumented Central American aliens throughout the United States and then to intern said Central American aliens in 10 military detention centers to be established during this Rex 84 readiness exercise:

(1) Fort Drum, New York, (2) Fort Indian town Gap, Penn., (3) A.P. Hill, Virginia, D.C., (4) Fort Benning, Georgia, (5) Eglin Air force Base, Florida, (6) Camp Crome, Florida, (FEMA/INS Administration/ Interrogation Center), (7) fort Chaffee, Arkansas, (8) Fort Huachuca, Arizona, (9) Egland Air Force Base, California, (10) Oakdale, California

To use the Minority leaders designated by the president in much the same manner in which we used Minority members who are agents with Central (CIA) and Federal (FBI) and we can not until there is no alternative reveal KING ALFRED in all its aspects. Minority members of congress will be unseated at once. This move is not without precedent in American history.

NATIONS ARE DESTROYED BECAUSE MEN FORGET

The Attorney General

Preliminary Memo: Department of Defense

    This memo is being submitted in lieu of a full report from the Joint Chiefs of Staff (JCS). That report is now in preparation. There will be many cities where the Minorities will be able to put into the street a superior number of people with a desperate and dangerous will. He will be formidable enemy, he is bound to the continent by heritage and knows that political asylum will not be available to him in other countries. The greatest concentration of the Minority is in the Deep South and Eastern Seaboard, the Great Lakes Region and the West Coast. While the national population exceeds that of the Minority by ten times, we must realistically take into account the following:

(1) An estimated 40 to 50% of the white population will not for various reasons engage the Minority during and Emergency, (2) American armed forces are spread around the world. A break out of war abroad means fewer troops at home to handle the Emergency, (3) local law enforcement officials must contain the Emergency until help arrives, though it may mean fighting a superior force. New York City for example, has a 25,000 man police force but there are about 1 million Minority members in the city. We are confident that the Minority can hold any city it took for only a few hours. The lack of weapons, facilities, logistics, all put the Minority at a final disadvantage.

Since the Korean War, this Department has shifted Minority members of the armed forces to combat to areas where combat is most likely to occur with the aim of eliminating through combat as many combat trained Minority servicemen as possible. Today the ratio of Minority member combat deaths in Vietnam where they are serving a "advisers" is twice as high as the Minority population ratio to the rest of America.

Below is the time table for KING ALFRED as tentatively suggested by the JCS who recommend that the operations be made over a period of eight (8) hours:

(1) Local police and Minorities leaders in action to head off the Emergency.

(2) Count-down to eight hours begins the moment the president determines the Emergency to be: [A] National, [B] Coordinated, [C] Of long duration, in the eighth Hour.

(3) County police join local police in the seventh hour.

(4) State police join county and local police in the sixth hour.

(5) Federal Marshals join state, county and local forces in the fifth hour.

(6) National Guards federalized, held in readiness in the forth hour.

(7) Regular armed forces alerted, take up positions. Minority troops divided and detained along with all white sympathizers under guard in the third hour.

(8) All Minority leaders, national and local detained in the second hour.

(9) President addresses the Minority or radio and television, gives it one hour to end the Emergency in the first hour.

Nations Are Destroyed Because Men Forget

(10) Zero hour, all units under Regional Commands into the Emergency.

Operational Committee Report:

Survey shows that during a six (6) year period, production created (million objects or 1,500,000 each year. Production could not dispose of the containers (bodies) which proved a bottle-neck. However, that was almost 20 years ago. We suggest vaporization (liquidation) techniques be employed to overcome production (extermination) problems inherent in KING ALFRED.

Secretary of Defense

Taken from the text of John Williams', "The Man Who Cried I Am". Having come into the information from unidentified government sources and felt it too controversial to release it directly to the general public but the entire document into a book he wrote.

At a later time the actual documents here obtained by other intelligence researchers, including Ms. May Britt, who forwarded to radio station KFJC, Los Altos Hills, California and was read over the air in September 1987. The first copies sent to KFJC never arrived. The third took over a week instead the average two days.

The exact wording of "THE KING ALFRED" document may or may not be word for word but it must be understood that the policy for such a program and plan does in fact exist within the National Security Council under the "REX 84" project authorized by Executive Order #52. Don't

NATIONS ARE DESTROYED BECAUSE MEN FORGET

say it can't happen here. IT IS HAPPENING!

Therefore, the Black Community must discuss this problem and must devise 'Contingency Plans' for our own survival locally, nationally, and globally.

They Thought They Were Following Elijah Muhammad, But Then It Was Too Late

As illustrated, these tactics were exercised on the peoples of Germany and now Americans; yet, one would be surprised to know that many of these same tactics had been used after the departure of Elijah Muhammad in 1975 and up to the current date while we speak. Sure it isn't demonstrated on the scale one had seen on these countries, but as we come to grip with what we actually are, we possibly will see differently. The Messenger said, "We are a nation. Get that in your mind." Once we get that fact in our minds and believe it, then re-examine the words and actions of our previous officials and there capitulation and collaboration, we will see just how much the information above relates to our status today as a nation. As long as we look at ourselves as simply a "black group, or a movement of sorts, we will be short changing ourselves.

This subject warrants a book all to its own and will be so titled as a sequel to this one title: **They Thought They Were Following Elijah Muhammad, But Then It Was Too Late** – Look for it!

MEMPS.COM

Thank you for purchasing this book. We trust the reading was rewarding and enlightening.

We offer various titles by Minister Nasir Hakim, as well a comprehensive collection of Messenger Elijah Muhammad's works. These works include, but are not limited to:

- **Standard Published Titles**
- Unpublished & Diligently Transcribed Compilations
- **Audio Cassettes**
- **Video Cassettes**
- **Audio CD's**
- **DVD's**
- **Rare Articles**
- **Year Books**
- **Annual Brochures**

You are welcomed to sample a catalog of these items by simply requesting a FREE archive Catalog.

Our contact information is as follows:
Secretarius MEMPS Publications
5025 North Central Avenue #415
Phoenix, Arizona 85012
Phone & Fax 602 466-7347
Email: cs@memps.com
Web: www.memps.com

Wholesale options are also available.

NATIONS ARE DESTROYED BECAUSE MEN FORGET